WHY DID THE FBI MONITOR MUHAMMAD ALI?

Josh Keen

London

Critical, Cultural and Communications Press

2020

A **CCCPress** paperback original.

Critical, Cultural and Communications Press is an imprint of
*Jet*stone Publishers Ltd.

ISBN 9781905510689

The right of Josh Keen to be identified as author in this work
has been asserted by him in accordance with the Copyright,
Designs and Patents Act, 1988.

Cover design by Hannibal.

Contents

Acknowledgements

I am very grateful to Miguel Hernandez for his guidance throughout this extensive research project. I also wish to express gratitude to the University of Exeter Library for their resources, as well as to my family and friends for continued support and counsel.

Foreword

This study seeks to explain the FBI's motivations for recording the activities of the late boxer Muhammad Ali between the period 1964-68. It will examine the Bureau's recently declassified (December 2016) files on Ali and outline the main factors which caused him to be considered politically subversive and worthy of such surveillance. By engaging with the historiography on the FBI, it will explore how perceptions of the federal agency have changed as its shield of secrecy has been gradually dissolved. Particular focus will be placed upon the overbearing influence on its activities of the Bureau's Director, J. Edgar Hoover, in particular in its counter-intelligence program. This study will show how Ali acted 'subversively' on multiple fronts, and how these must therefore be seen in the context of Hoover's own personal beliefs about what America should look like and what sort of behaviour could be tolerated.

Exploring the FBI's reaction to Ali's involvement in the 'semi-religious group', the Nation of Islam, will reveal Hoover's anxieties over Ali's devotion to Elijah Muhammad's interpretation of Islam, as well as his radical standpoint on race relations. This study will also engage briefly with accounts so far produced of the Ali files and present their limitations in understating the importance of Ali's role as heavyweight champion in intensifying the Bureau's fears about Ali's beliefs. Finally, analysis of the correlation between FBI surveillance and Ali's increasingly public anti-Vietnam War stance will highlight the chief significance of Ali's politically symbolic refusal to join the armed forces and of the movement that he stirred.

A Note on the FBI Archive

The FBI files on Muhammad Ali discussed in this study can be read online at **https://vault.fbi.gov/muhammad-ali**. Not all of the documents on Ali are yet available and many of those which are have been redacted (i.e. they have some information erased) but I hope this short examination of these sources will prompt further research on this extraordinary archive.

The files were released in four batches. They do not appear to be arranged in any immediately apparent chronological or thematic sequence. Each scanned page in the archive was given a 'Bates number' (consisting of the suffix 'Muhammad Ali-' then a 3- or 4-figure digit) in the bottom right corner, and within each batch these numbers always ascend. The documents appear in the four batches as follows:

Batch 1   Pages 346-514 (142 pages with unnumbered first page)
Batch 2   Pages 515-1016 (465 pages)
Batch 3   Pages 257-1315 (296 pages)
Batch 4   Pages 761-890 (36 pages)

As can be seen from the page counts, which do not tally with the page ranges, hundreds of presumably existing pages were not released in the published archive (no accessible page has a Bates number lower than 257, and the available archive amounts to a total of 939 pages despite the highest Bates-numbered accessible page being 1315).

In the footnote references in this study I have assigned the Ali FBI archive the abbreviation 'AFBIA' followed by the document batch and Bates-numbered pages being cited. Thus, for example, 'AFBIA 2, 967' means batch 2, Bates-numbered page 'Muhammad Ali-967'.

Introduction

Muhammad Ali was America.
Muhammad Ali will always be America. [1]

So said Valerie Jarrett, reading a tribute from U.S. President Barack Obama and his wife Michelle at Ali's funeral in 2016. Rarely had an athlete received such universal appreciation and adoration as did Muhammad Ali at the time of his passing. The former boxer, once Cassius Marcellus Clay, Jr., was revered as perhaps the greatest competitor and showman of his generation. White and black journalists celebrated Ali's life 'as if they had been in his corner all along'.[2] Ali, in truth, had been a polarising figure and, in contrast with Obama's assertion, had not been perceived to incarnate America. His views on race and religion were radical in the 1960s U.S.A. and were met with searing criticism. Such opposition was no better encapsulated than in the response of the then Director of the FBI, J. Edgar Hoover. The FBI Director monitored Ali extensively as part of the Bureau's secret 'Counter Intelligence Program' or 'COINTELPRO'. It sought to undermine groups and individuals judged to be 'subversive', a term encompassing a broad range of dissident political activities.[3]

---

[1] Brendan Smialowski, 'Obama's statement read at Ali funeral: "Muhammad Ali was America"', *theScore*, 10 June 2016, available at **https://thesco.re/2KlAq4N** (accessed 18 April 2018).

[2] Stephen Townsend, 'From "Pitifully Ignorant" to the "People's Champion": Shifting Perceptions of Muhammad Ali in the Louisville Defender, 1964-1971', *Kentucky Historical Society* 115, 4 (2017), 638.

[3] Athan Theoharis, *From the Secret Files of J. Edgar Hoover* (Chicago: Ivan R. Dee, 1993), 86.

This study seeks to show why Ali attracted such obsessive surveillance from the agency, relying upon the FBI files on Ali as the primary focus of its research. The hysteria surrounding Ali's 1971 bout against Joe Frazier provided a distraction for the burglary by eight activists who broke into an FBI office in Pennsylvania. It sparked revelations about Hoover's spying operations which included the collection of information on Ali. Since 1974, increasingly more FBI files have been obtained through the Freedom of Information Act (FOIA). However, it was not until 2016 that the agency's files on Ali were more abundantly divulged and the full extent of its investigation into Ali came to light. The documents were released in response to an FOIA lawsuit by the conservative group Judicial Watch, launched in August 2016, shortly after Ali's death.[4] Files were uploaded to the Bureau's website in batches, the first on 2 December 2016, and the last on 21 January 2017. Judicial Watch's intention was not to criticise the agency's treatment of Ali, though the nearly 1,000 pages of documents do shed light on the prejudice and illegality with which it followed him. Some documents date from as late as 1978, though this study's focus is on COINTELPRO activities under Hoover's leadership. While the program extended to 1971, and Hoover's tenure to 2 May 1972, there are few available files pertaining to the years 1969-72, or concerning an investigation into a threat made against 'well known Negroes' among whom Ali was included but rarely discussed.[5] My study contends that Hoover's values shaped the Bureau's activities during the period in which they

[4] David Bixenspan, 'Muhammad Ali's FBI Files released after Conservative Group's Lawsuit', *Law & Crime*, 16 December 2016, available at **https://bit.ly/2reswCs** (accessed 11 December 2017).
[5] AFBIA 2, 967.

surveilled Ali. The FBI director held a distinct socio-political vision of how America should look, to which Ali did not conform in multiple respects.

Chapter 1 engages with the existing literature on the FBI in order for this study to position itself within that scholarship. Only recently, through the ability of historians, journalists and political activists 'to pierce the screen of secrecy which formerly immunized FBI records from scrutiny', have we discovered the scope and targets of COINTELPRO surveillance. [6] I assess the utility of works written prior to this increased transparency, particularly the image that they ascribed to Hoover. I also examine histories produced after the enactment of the FOIA, part of a developing field, as files like Ali's are only just being released.

The agency claimed to have kept tabs on the late boxer as part of its investigation to 'show Ali's relationship with the Nation of Islam' (NOI), although this study posits a more multifaceted explanation. Chapter 2 engages with the limited existing literature about the files, arguing that it overlooks the importance of Ali himself in attracting FBI surveillance, and that it places too strong an emphasis on his membership within the NOI. I acknowledge that Ali's embrace of its quasi-religious doctrine was a concern to Hoover. Moreover, Ali's devotion to Islam ultimately informed his racial views, for which Hoover displayed greater contempt. His rejection of racial integration pushed Ali's radicalism beyond that of famous civil rights leaders like Martin Luther King, Jr., who himself was a major target of Hoover's COINTELPRO. However, the chapter asserts that the current literature fails to account for the extent of Hoover's obsession with Ali: the

[6] Athan G. Theoharis, 'Dissent and the State: Unleashing the FBI, 1917-1985', *The History Teacher* 24, 1 (1990), 49.

FBI tracked everything from his divorce proceedings to traffic fines, despite insisting that he was not personally under investigation. It is significant that the Bureau saw Ali as worthy of such extensive state surveillance, despite not even being part of the NOI leadership. Ali's status as a heavyweight boxing champion cannot be disregarded, as 'No sooner did Clay win the title than he moved off the sports page and on to the front page'.[7] Americans historically viewed their heavyweight champions as proud emblems of their nation. Ali, however, emphatically subverted traditional expectations. Consequently, 'every competition, every success, was a veritable political statement against the white status quo', which Hoover protected.[8]

The teachings of Elijah Muhammad, known as 'the Messenger', were adjudged by Hoover to be anti-American. The files contain suspicions and criticisms of Ali's religious and racial views, but Chapter 3 contends that it was Ali's political statements – particularly his draft refusal – which generated the most surveillance. The majority of Ali's files fall in 1966, when he was seeking conscientious-objector status. He maintained that his conscience precluded him from participating in the Vietnam conflict at a time shortly after the Kennedy Administration had 'quickly conveyed an image of dynamism and purpose in foreign affairs'.[9] Ali directly

[7] Randy Roberts, 'The Politics and Economics of Televised Boxing', in Elliot J. Gorn (ed.), *Muhammad Ali: The People's Champ* (Urbana: University of Illinois Press, 1995), 42.

[8] Gerald Early, 'Some Preposterous Propositions from the Heroic Life of Muhammad Ali: A Reading of *The Greatest: My Own Story*', in Gorn, *Muhammad Ali*, 80.

[9] Thomas R. Hietala, 'Ali and the Age of Bare-Knuckle Politics', in Gorn, *Muhammad Ali*, 123.

undermined this notion, stating 'I don't have no personal quarrel with those Viet Congs', a quotation increasingly circulated (not always with accuracy) as anti-war sentiment rose.[10] Ali was perceived by Hoover to be traitorous, and it was consequently his becoming a symbol of the anti-war movement that transformed him into a significant political dissident.[11]

---

[10] Leigh Montville, *Sting Like a Bee: Muhammad Ali vs. The United States of America, 1966-1971* (New York: Anchor Books, 2017), 23.
[11] Hietala, 'Ali and the Age of Bare-Knuckle Politics', 124.

Chapter 1
The FBI's attack on domestic dissent

Scholarship on the FBI did not gain credibility until after 1974, when access to some of the Bureau's files was obtained through the FOIA. The literature that came before can almost all be treated as primary source material, reflections of the baleful influence that Hoover wielded over the agency and its monitoring of figures like Muhammad Ali. Authors were faced with the restrictive situation of supporting the Bureau in return for use of its files, or producing critical accounts whose reliance on outside information – commonly from resentful former agents – discredited them. The consequence was a collection of 'laudatory pieces that parroted the output of the agency's extensive public relations (PR) apparatus', and can be seen as an extension of FBI propaganda. [1] Courtney Rule Cooper's preliminary account on the Bureau introduced the 'FBI formula' in lauding its efficacy and rectitude.[2] His book was personally ratified by Hoover, as was Don Whitehead's *The FBI Story*, which similarly reinforced the accepted, Bureau-authored canon. [3] Whitehead gained comprehensive access to FBI files, but this was in exchange for his guarantee to Hoover that Hoover could personally enforce changes to his text where he judged them necessary. Whitehead's 'objective' book consequently distorted the Bureau's history, omitting, for example, FBI agent Melvin Purvis from the shooting of Dillinger – 'the Bureau's defining

[1] William J. Vizzard, 'The FBI, A Hundred-Year Retrospective', *Public Administration Review* 68, 6 (2008), 1079.

[2] Courtney Ryley Cooper, *Ten Thousand Public Enemies* (Boston: Little, Brown and Co., 1935).

[3] Don Whitehead, *The FBI Story: A Report to the People* (New York: Cop, 1956).

early moment'.[4]

Following Hoover's death in 1972, and increasing public demand for transparency from intelligence agencies, a new era of critical literature ensued. Revelations of COINTELPRO spotlighted unethical activity, and as for the notion of 'Hoover as a protector of civil liberties, the historical record is unequivocal in its judgement of the falsehood of that claim'.[5] The narrative hence shifted away from the depiction of the 'one dimensional, heroic "G-men" braving danger on behalf of their impeccable Director', to one that considered the constitutional guarantees that Hoover's boys undermined.[6] The Bureau was a relatively uncontrolled agency that had dedicated more resources to policing political thought than acting as the country's foremost crime-fighting agency.

Memoirs of former Bureau leaders coincided with this newly prevailing literature. Despite being rather personalised narratives, collectively they substantiate commonly asserted theories about FBI malpractice, and Hoover's centrality to it. William C. Sullivan's posthumous autobiography provides a firm critique of Hoover's leadership, documenting the issues of a 'governmental agency operat[ing] virtually as a private preserve by its "Director"'.[7] There remains the possibility that

[4] Matthew Cecil, *Hoover's FBI and the Fourth Estate: The Campaign to Control the Press and the Bureau's Image* (Lawrence: University Press of Kansas, 2014), 14.

[5] Matthew Cecil, *The Ballad of Ben and Stella Mae: Great Plains Outlaws Who Became FBI Public Enemies Nos. 1 and 2* (Lawrence: University Press of Kansas, 2017), 60.

[6] Melissa Graves, 'FBI Historiography', in C. R. Moran and J. Christopher (eds.), *Intelligence Studies in Britain and the US* (Edinburgh: Edinburgh University Press, 2013), 129.

[7] Irvin Karg, 'Review Article: *The Bureau: My Thirty Years in*

Sullivan inflated Hoover's role in order to deflect blame, though his intimate perspective as the third highest ranking official in the FBI lends his account authority. Moreover, former agent Joseph L. Schott's *No Left Turns* corroborates his assertions about Hoover's supremacy, despite a contrasting perspective, that is, one removed from the Bureau's leadership. Schott recalls the internal culture of the agency as defined by the 'god-like reign' of its Director, which deterred any agent's rebellious dissent. [8] That such a culture existed within both the leadership and rank-and-file of the Bureau, in which those whose views differed from Hoover's were shunned, it is unsurprising that he maintained the same policy externally, by silencing those who, like Ali, rebelled against his personal belief system.

Whitehead's history conformed to the standard rendering of an agency under Hoover that embraced evolution, writing that 'the history of the FBI, in reality, is the story of America itself and the struggle for an ideal'.[9] In reality, COINTELPRO underlined Hoover's opposition to change, his clinging on to what he saw as traditional societal values by attempting to control political diversity within the U.S.A. Galen Roger Perras criticises Rhodri Jeffreys-Jones's overemphasis of FBI shortcomings, but he ultimately concedes that Hoover 'took advantage of circumstances [...] to advance its particular interests'. [10] If President Roosevelt's original purpose in

Hoover's F.B.I., by William C. Sullivan and Bill Brown', *American Bar Association Journal* 67, 1 (1981), 72.

[8] Joseph L. Schott, *No Left Turns* (New York: Ballantine Books, 1975), 2-5.

[9] Whitehead, *The FBI Story*, 323.

[10] Galen Roger Perras, 'Review Article: *The FBI: A History*, by Rhodri Jeffreys-Jones', *Social History* 42, 93 (2009), 254-5.

expanding the FBI's capacity to monitor dissent derived from a mistrust over foreign-directed activities, 'he had unwittingly opened a Pandora's box'.[11] The FBI, rather than enacting the will of Congress, instead developing its own agenda, as defined by Hoover. The agency sought to disenfranchise individuals and groups it deemed 'subversive' through covert operations intended to 'reap dissension and disunion'.[12]

Ali's so-called 'dissent' therefore must be seen in the context of Hoover's idea of social order. The Bureau even resorted to illegal and improper means to gather information, including 'surreptitious entries, illegal wiretaps, and other electronic surveillance, and it distorted the information it collected'.[13] Douglas M. Charles's recent work, *The FBI's Obscene File*, fills a gap in prior historiography. He explores the Bureau's attempts to 'control obscenity according to Hoover's personal agendas'.[14] The FBI's operation against illicit material, Charles contends, ran in parallel with American social values. His study offers a microcosmic example of the Bureau more broadly 'operating against that, which the country, as a whole, found unacceptable'.[15] However, Hoover's moulding of public opinion cannot be understated. Both Ali and the NOI were far from widely

[11] Theoharis, 'Dissent and the State', 44.

[12] Graves, 'FBI Historiography', 136.

[13] Matthew Cecil, *Branding Hoover's FBI: How the Boss's PR Men Sold the Bureau to America* (Lawrence: University Press of Kansas, 2016), 261.

[14] Reba Kennedy, 'Review Article: *The FBI's Obscene File: J. Edgar Hoover and the Bureau's Crusade against Smut*, by Douglas M. Charles', *Library Journal* 137, 10 (2012), 114.

[15] Graves, 'FBI Historiography', 140.

adored, and the FBI seized opportunities when possible to smear them. Moreover, as Matthew Cecil writes, successful propaganda 'would result in an audience of people who essentially chose to incorporate the organisation's preferred understandings of itself as an element of their own identities'. Subsequently, the Bureau by its own efforts, became a reflection of conservative American opinion, and 'an attack on Hoover's FBI [...] would be an attack on the mainstream Americans'. [16]

Without exception, each COINTELPRO was implemented solely on the authority of an internal memorandum initiated by Hoover. Scholars have written about numerous forms of dissident behaviour against which Hoover launched counter-intelligence tactics. Perhaps the most well documented is the FBI's political crusade against communism, particularly directed against the American Communist Party. Kenneth O'Reilly contends that the FBI's propaganda, was 'more [important] than the efforts of any other anticommunist group'.[17] O'Reilly argues that the Bureau had a dominant role in American politics, employing propaganda to enforce a specific vision of what it meant to be an American, including a fierce opposition to communism. Conversely, as Jeffreys-Jones sees it, race served more as the backdrop to the FBI's COINTELPRO. He argues that the Bureau has 'reason to be proud of its origins', owing to its work aimed at protecting African American rights at the turn of the century. [18]

---

[16] Cecil, *Branding Hoover's FBI*, 5.

[17] Kenneth O'Reilly, *Hoover and the Un-Americans: The FBI, HUAC, and the Red Menace* (Philadelphia: Temple University Press, 1983), 8.

[18] Rhodri Jeffreys-Jones, *The FBI: A History* (New Haven: Yale University Press, 2007), 5.

However, he equally stresses that the FBI abandoned its progressive stance on race, evidenced most clearly by Hoover's diatribe against the Civil Rights Movement.

John Drabble comments that there has been a lack of scholarship on the FBI's work against a Ku Klux Klan (KKK) revival, as well as its combating of other racist organisations like the American Nazi Party, because scholarship on COINTELPRO has been restricted to 'operations against civil rights, black nationalists, and New Leftist groups'. [19] However, such actions are undermined by their motivations: The Klan resurgence was a 'potential threat to Hoover's cherished relations with local law enforcers'. [20] Thus, such activities are not inconsistent with the FBI morphing into a representation of Hoover's own traditional middle-class white attitudes, within which racism was inherent.

Instead of accentuating a particular anxiety of Hoover's, evidence on the FBI's pursuit of Muhammad Ali allies itself more with David J. Garrow's broader 'cultural threat' thesis. His argument is that 'the essence of the Bureau's social role has been not to attack critics, Communists, black or leftists per se, but to repress all perceived threats to the dominant status-quo oriented political culture'. [21] Hoover ultimately feared change and worked to maintain the 'status quo', so any attack upon it – in Ali's case, religious, social, and political – was deemed a threat towards 'Americanity' or the 'American civil religion'. 'Americanity' reflected the semi-religious

[19] John Drabble, 'The FBI, COINTELPRO-WHITE HATE, and the Decline of Ku Klux Klan Organisations in Alabama, 1964-1971', *Alabama Review* 61, 1 (2008), 4.

[20] Jeffreys-Jones, *The FBI*, 172.

[21] David J. Garrow, *The FBI and Martin Luther King, Jr.: From 'Solo' to Memphis* (New York: Penguin Books, 1983), 208.

aspect of the idea of America as a 'melting pot' in which immigrants should adopt new identities as Americans.[22] As discussed by Robert N. Bellah in his essay on the American civil religion, biblical themes are evoked within the U.S.A.'s historiography:

> Americans are viewed as the 'chosen people'; Benjamin Franklin and George Washington resemble prophets; it even has sacred events like the Declaration of Independence, and symbols like the Statue of Liberty and the White House.[23]

Gardell reasons that the United States and FBI were viewed as defenders of moral decency against every form of corruptibility, which 'during the Cold War was principally defined as communism but is now increasingly replaced by Islam'.[24] Ultimately, the Bureau was a largely homogenous organisation, which selected personnel from conservative and mainstream backgrounds who were willing to defend 'good old America'. The NOI and Muhammad Ali, by this account, were seen as 'un-American', and thus targets for counter-intelligence actions.[25]

As I go on to argue, the FBI files demonstrate that the NOI

---

[22] Mattias Gardell, *In the Name of Elijah Muhammad: Louis Farrakhan and the Nation of Islam* (Durham, NC: Duke University Press, 1996), 93.

[23] Robert N. Bellah, 'Civil Religion in America', *Journal of American Academy of Arts and Sciences* 134, 4 (2006), 40-55, quoted in Gardell, *In the Name of Elijah Muhammad*, 93-4.

[24] Gardell, *In the Name of Elijah Muhammad*, 94.

[25] Richard Brent Turner, *Islam in the African American Experience* (Bloomington: Indiana University Press, 2003), 45.

was a significant impetus to the enactment of a policy of monitoring Ali. However, Gardell complains that there has been a lack of research focusing directly on the federal conspiracy against the NOI.[26] Instead, the history of the NOI has been cast under the more general narrative of American domestic repression. Furthermore, even aside from the FBI, the scholarship on the NOI has been largely 'reactionary in nature', overly concerned with the sensationalist aspects of the group.[27] Malcolm X has undoubtedly received the most scholarly attention, which overlooks the effect of others like the Honourable Elijah Muhammad, who attracted a great deal of scrutiny from Hoover's counter-intelligence program. It is only since the 1990s that Muhammad has received more recognition by historians: he is an important figure and central to the FBI's investigations of Ali.[28] As Dawn-Marie Gibson comments, it was the 'proselytizing efforts of Muhammad and his ministers' that contributed to the NOI's exponential growth, which ultimately drew the attention of the FBI.[29] Scholarly research on the NOI in the 1990s benefited from the declassification of FBI surveillance files on the group and its leaders.

These files demonstrate that, as Muhammad's movement grew, the Bureau 'matched the subsequent growth of the

[26] Gardell, *In the Name of Elijah Muhammad*, 71.

[27] Dawn-Marie Gibson, *A History of the Nation of Islam: Race, Islam, and the Quest for Freedom* (Santa Barbara: Praeger, 2012), ix.

[28] Key works include: Claude Andrew Clegg, *An Original Man: the Life and Times of Elijah Muhammad* (New York: St Martin's Press, 1997); and Karl Evanzz, *The Messenger: the Rise and Fall of Elijah Muhammad* (New York: Pantheon Books, 1999).

[29] Gibson, *A History of the Nation of Islam*, 27.

Nation by an extended program of surveillance'.[30] Thus, it was not just Malcolm X who gained enough limelight to capture the attention of Hoover's boys, who sought to neutralize the group. The Messenger's religious and racial teachings promoted a version of Islam which stressed 'African pride, discipline, and self-sufficiency', and were at odds with the patriotic values of 'Americanity' espoused by Hoover's agency.[31]

While some historians have explored the impact of and reception to Muhammad, Malcolm, and the NOI more generally, Johnny Smith comments that no academic historian has written a biography on Muhammad Ali's life. This gap is bemusing as historians have written treatments of black heavyweight champions Jack Johnson and Joe Louis, both of whom also had a significant cultural impact outside of the ring. Moreover, academic histories of the 1960s and the Black Freedom Movement have either excluded Ali's influence or 'compartmentaliz[ed] him in the history of sports'. However, Ali's cultural footprint was immense, and this is reflected by the FBI's fixation. 'Ali's career as a boxer offers historians a link between the Black Freedom Movement, the Vietnam War, and popular culture', making him perhaps the ultimate 'cultural threat' to the conservative values that the Bureau fought to maintain. [32] Ali's public stand in support of the NOI made him a target for mainstream American rage. While the Congress passed the

[30] Gardell, *In the Name of Elijah Muhammad*, 71.

[31] Rob Shone, *Muhammad Ali: The Life of a Boxing Hero* (New York: Rosen Central, 2007), 7.

[32] Johnny Smith, 'Reflections: Remembering Muhammad Ali: Myths, Memory, and History', *Reviews in American History* 45, 1 (2017), 178.

Civil Rights Act in 1964, the most sweeping piece of legislative racial integration, 'Ali joined a group whose appeal centred around black separatism'.[33]

The release of the FBI's files on Ali is hugely significant. Gardell admits that his account of the FBI's covert actions against the NOI, like others, 'can at best be seen as a rough delineation'.[34] However, while many recent scholarly works on the NOI stop short of providing an analysis of Ali's membership in and significance to it, these files show just how essential he was. Moreover, aside from the NOI, the files highlight that Ali seemed to epitomise Hoover's ultimate dissident: his religion, separatist views on race, and stand against the Vietnam War, magnified by the famed position of heavyweight champion he occupied, signalled a considerable anxiety for Hoover. It is 'difficult to document, quantify, or clearly express the influence that fear of his [Hoover's] control of informants generated', [35] but the files on Ali contribute considerably to our knowledge of the FBI in this period and the extent to which Hoover shaped the Bureau.

[33] Benjamin T. Harrison, 'The Muhammad Ali Draft Case and Public Debate on the Vietnam War', *Peace Research* 33, 2 (2001), 72.
[34] Gardell, *In the Name of Elijah Muhammad*, 72.
[35] Cecil, *Branding Hoover's FBI*, 2.

Chapter 2

Islam, 'Black Power', and the self-determination of a black heavyweight champion

Scholars have yet to scrutinize Ali's FBI files, so the existing literature is purely journalistic. Their assessments seem hurried, often referring to just a handful of documents, not allowing for a full analysis. Journalists have characterised the files as merely an extension of the FBI's probe into the NOI. *The New York Times* dispensed the headline, 'F.B.I. Monitored Muhammad Ali Connections to Nation of Islam', while *Sky News* reported, 'FBI papers reveal watch on Muhammad Ali over Nation of Islam links'. However, the files themselves reveal broader motivations.[1] This chapter considers the role Ali's NOI membership performed in spurring Hoover's obsessive surveillance. It also looks beyond Ali simply being another member of the movement, and assesses the unique exposure and finance that Ali furnished for the NOI. Lastly, Ali's rebellion against white conservative expectations of a heavyweight champion is examined.

While Ali's NOI membership did not solely account for the Bureau's watch on him, it undoubtedly contributed. According to the files, their interest in the NOI did not commence with Ali, as the organisation had been under 'continuous investigation by this Bureau for a number of years'.[2] Hoover had closely followed Elijah and Herbert

[1] Victor Mather, 'F.B.I Monitored Muhammad Ali Connections to Nation of Islam', *The New York Times*, 15 December 2016, available at **https://nyti.ms/2JhRBTH** (accessed 11 February 2018); Anonymous, 'FBI papers reveal watch on Muhammad Ali over Nation of Islam links', *Sky News*, 16 December 2016, available at **https://bit.ly/2qRfGtH** (accessed 11 February 2018).
[2] AFBIA 1, 412.

Muhammad as part of a 'program to disrupt organisations [...] considered subversive'. [3] The FBI's Security Index, a listing of prominent dissidents dating from 1939, also supports the interpretation that Ali was the latest addition to a list of NOI 'subversives'. The largest category listed 673 members of the NOI, compared to 476 communists, which shows that being a NOI member was seen as a form of 'dissidence' as profound, or perhaps more profound, than communism. [4] The group was viewed as a radical sect by nearly all, so 'Ali's membership [...] frightened white Americans and divided black Americans, too'. [5]

Hoover's boys displayed interest not only in Ali's membership but also the nature of it. A single informant issued seven reports in the space of a month concerning Ali's role within the NOI, and whether or not he held a position of authority. [6] The FBI received confirmation via an airtel (an outdated data communication process used internally within the FBI) in March 1966 that Muhammad had addressed Ali's attendance at the Annual Muslim Convention and said, 'He won't be up on no speaker's stand. He's no minister.' [7] However, five months later, a source advised the agency that Ali 'was referred to by an official of that organisation [NOI] as a Minister', underlining that the anxiety over his membership had not dissipated. [8] The NOI factor is further exemplified by the significant portion of the files dedicated to

[3] Jonathan Eig, *Ali: A Life* (London: Simon and Schuster, 2017), 178.
[4] Kenneth O'Reilly, *'Racial Matters': The FBI's Secret File on Black America, 1960-1972* (New York: Macmillan, 1989), 275.
[5] Smith, 'Remembering Muhammad Ali', 183.
[6] AFBIA 1, 405.
[7] *Ibid.*, 406.
[8] *Ibid.*, 486.

disrupting the group. C. D. Brennan, an assistant director of the Intelligence Division, informed William Sullivan that the NOI's leadership was planning on 'arrang[ing] a marriage between his show piece and the dowdy daughter of a Muslim sub-boss'. [9] Their interest, however, did not lie with Ali's personal life, but rather that 'if furnished to and publicised by a nationally syndicated columnist, [it] could embarrass and disrupt' the NOI.[10] Thus, in certain records, while Ali figured, the priority was to exploit journalists' cooperation and undermine the allegedly subversive NOI.

Hoover's interest in Ali's NOI involvement was grounded in the radical beliefs the group inspired, which threatened the United States' 'internal security'.[11] Ali's adherence to Islam was seen to challenge white conservative Christian standards.[12] The Bureau's files often referred to the NOI as 'The Black Muslims', because the term 'Muslim' was considered derogatory and often equated with dissidence.[13] Ali himself protested at the label: 'You call it Black Muslims, I don't. The real name is Islam. That means peace. Yet people brand us a hate group.'[14] Hoover 'was a man of high principle whose beliefs were based on Christian faith', and noted that Ali had spoken out against 'this hocus-pocus religion, Christianity'.[15] Ali challenged Christian theology, a bulwark

[9] AFBIA 2, 516.

[10] *Ibid.*

[11] AFBIA 1, 348.

[12] Arash Markazi, 'Muhammad Ali a champion for his faith until the end', *ABC News*, 10 June 2016, available at **https://abcn.ws/ 2HgypsU** (accessed 12 March 2018).

[13] AFBIA 1, 358.

[14] Eig, *Ali: A Life*, 154.

[15] Ray Wannall, *The Real J. Edgar Hoover: For the Record*

of the American civil religion. Jack Olsen's article in *Sports Illustrated*, which Hoover's boys keenly recorded, stated that 'Muhammad's book *Message to the Blackman*, is studied by Cassius like a Bible'.[16] Olsen's simile is ironic, as Muhammad's book is the antithesis to what Hoover saw as the sacrosanct Christian text. The FBI had informants advising on a planned tour through Europe, as it provided a platform for Ali to repeat Muhammad's religious rhetoric, but agents advised that Muhammad was 'primarily concerned with purchasing Sts. Constantine and Helen Greek Orthodox Church' in Chicago.[17] This literal and symbolic replacing of Christianity by Muhammad's Islam was a worry for the Bureau.

Hoover's religious anxiety meant that he was alerted to any build-up before Ali's fights that perchance reflected his faith. They recorded the 19 July 1964 issue of the *Courier-Journal* newspaper, in which Ali was quoted as saying, 'I want Floyd Patterson. He insulted my religion and I wanted to get at him.'[18] Many observed the fight as a clash between Islam and Christianity – Malcom X even called it 'the Cross and the Crescent fighting in a prize ring' – an opportunity seen by Hoover's boys for Islam to be thwarted.[19]

The Bureau's enthusiasm did not cease at Ali's professional career: its religious concerns manifested themselves in close attention to Ali's divorce proceedings. The Miami

(Paducah: Turner Publishing Company), 204; AFBIA 2, 583.
[16] Jack Olsen, 'A Case of Conscience', *Sports Illustrated*, 11 April 1966, in AFBIA 1, 423.
[17] AFBIA 2, 610.
[18] *Ibid.*, 619.
[19] Malcolm X and Alex Haley, *The Autobiography of Malcolm X as told to Alex Haley* (New York: Ballantine Books, 1992), 354.

Office sent article clippings from the *Miami Daily* newspaper to Hoover concerning 'CASSIUS CLAY'S recent divorce from SONYA CLAY'.[20] The FBI was absorbed by the religious implications of the divorce: Ali's wife 'hadn't lived up to the Muslim faith'.[21] Her lipstick and dress were at odds with the modest values of the NOI. Moreover, the Bureau merely repeated a gossip item from *Jet Magazine*, which fashioned an unfounded rumour that Ali might be wedding 'one of the daughters of United Arab Republic President GAMAL ADBEL NASSER'.[22] The FBI saw it worthy to file nonetheless, highlighting the fear that Ali might wed a Muslim woman.

However, 'for many young and rebellious black people, Ali's religion didn't matter', the important facet to Ali's non-conformity being his advocacy of Black Power.[23] The FBI defined the NOI as an 'all Negro, semireligious antiwhite organisation'.[24] The lexical choice of 'semireligious' shows that the FBI viewed them more as a racially politicised group. While Islamophobia was a preoccupation of the agency, it was more concerned with the racial commentary within Muhammad's interpretation of Islam. The FBI saw Ali's change of name as a demonstration of his 'unflinching loyalty to the racist Muslim Nation of Islam'.[25] It represented a critique on race relations in America, with Ali urging mental emancipation from the 'slave names' administered by white people.[26] FBI agents continually referred to Ali as 'Cassius Clay' despite

[20] AFBIA 1, 381.
[21] *Ibid.*
[22] *Ibid.*, 510.
[23] Eig, *Ali: A Life*, 216.
[24] AFBIA 1, 412.
[25] AFBIA 2, 582.
[26] *Ibid.*

being fully aware that Muhammad Ali had become his legal name, emphasising their objection to his challenge to the American racial hierarchy. Moreover, Ali argued that African Americans were subjected to the 'false religion of Christianity' in order 'to keep the so-called Negro thinking white'.[27]

The FBI's most marked objection was to Ali's preaching of anti-integration. When asked in 1964 what he meant by 'real freedom', the FBI noted that Ali's response was, 'The only freedom we can really have is separation.'[28] Montville asserts that the NOI's separation discourse pushed them 'closer to the teachings of the KKK than the work of Reverend Martin Luther King'.[29] The views Ali upheld were not seen simply as activism but as innate racism and, given the FBI's history of endeavouring to undermine the KKK, it is no wonder that they adopted similar measures to disrupt 'racism' against whites. The extremism of separation was not felt just by whites: even Ali's local newspaper, *The Louisville Defender*, admonished him. While it determinedly pursued black equality, it did so through 'accommodationist tactics that did not conform with the more aggressive stance adopted by Ali, the Nation of Islam'.[30]

Ali essentially echoed the Messenger's racial cries for America to fall and be rebuilt, which was anathema to the traditionalist views of Hoover, who wished to retain social structures and beliefs from the 1940s and 1950s. Rather than subscribe to the FBI's vision of 'Americanity', which demands that immigrants accept their American status while being governed by the dominant white institutions, Ali spelled out

[27] *Ibid.*, 584.

[28] *Ibid.*, 618.

[29] Montville, *Sting Like a Bee*, 16.

[30] Townsend, 'Shifting Perceptions of Muhammad Ali', 617.

an aggressive opposition. Certain sections of the Messenger's book were described to Hoover, within which 'The dominant theme [...] is hatred of the whites'.[31] A particular focus was on Ali's threat of a 'War of Armageddon' that would topple the white institution and culminate in the elimination of whites.[32] The FBI equated this anti-white sentiment with anti-Americanism, and nowhere was it more explicit than in Elijah Muhammad reportedly saying, 'America will fall', according to a *Sports Illustrated* article.[33]

Moreover, FBI agents stated that Muhammad's followers believed 'the so-called Negroes are slaves of the white race, referred to as "white devils"'.[34] 'White devils' is a commonly repeated refrain throughout the files, because the FBI was troubled by Ali's suggestion that America was run by 'devils'. The racial prejudice of the agency ran deep, even to the extreme of its threatening Martin Luther King, Jr. for campaigning for civil rights. However, while King preached non-violence, Ali preferred the NOI's notion of self-defence: 'if you hit me, I'll hit you back'.[35] The FBI's anxiety over violent tactics was reflected by their extensive search into whether Ali was a member of the Fruit of Islam (FOI), the NOI's paramilitary wing. Agents initially concluded that 'Clay is definitely not a captain in the FOI and his wearing the uniform was only honorary'.[36] However, after the Senior

[31] Olsen, 'A Case of Conscience', in AFBIA 1, 423.

[32] AFBIA 1, 495.

[33] Olsen, 'A Case of Conscience', in AFBIA 1, 423.

[34] AFBIA 1, 495.

[35] Anonymous, 'How Muhammad Ali found home in Nation of Islam and why he embraced the religion', *Hindustan Times*, 9 June 2016, available at **http://bit.ly/2G3B9Iz** (accessed 12 February 2018).

[36] AFBIA 1, 355.

Officer in Charge (SAC) of Chicago learned that Ali had placed an order for an FOI captain's uniform, the investigation was heightened to determine if he 'actually holds a position of authority in the NOI', as this would determine 'whether or not CLAY should be considered for the Security Index' – a list of individuals thought to be endangering national security.[37]

In spite of journalists' accounts, Ali was in fact monitored for more than just being a member of the NOI and advancing its views. Surveillance also entailed recording what he delivered to the NOI: Ali was both a potential source of publicity and money, 'a galvanizing force, and him running around free was a problem for the FBI'. [38] An unnamed informant warned that Ali would be a 'gold mine' for those handling him, an issue for Hoover given his aversion to the NOI.[39]

Besides Malcom X, 'none of Elijah Muhammad's disciples gave the NOI a higher visibility than Muhammad Ali'.[40] The attention Ali garnered, coupled with his acceptance of Muhammad's authority over his life, meant that the FBI was concerned that Ali was becoming 'his protégé', as reported by a *Louisville Times* article which agents recorded.[41] While its investigation of Ali's FOI affiliation may initially have been racially motivated, the Bureau was informed that Ali wore the

---

[37] *Ibid.*, 403.

[38] Michael Ezra, telephone interview, quoted in Alex Dobuzinskis, 'FBI kept tabs on Muhammad Ali in 1966 during Nation of Islam probe', Reuters, 16 December 2016, available at **http://reut.rs/ 2yYv5uu** (accessed 11 December 2018)

[39] AFBIA 4, 874.

[40] Gardell, *In the Name of Elijah Muhammad*, 67.

[41] Edmund J. Rooney, 'FBI Watches Black Muslim, Cassius Clay', *Louisville Times*, in AFBIA 1, 354.

captain's uniform due to 'an honorary title bestowed on him because of his publicity value to the NOI'. [42] The FBI considered Ali as a public relations vehicle for Muhammad, who it thought was honouring him not because of his devout commitment to Islam, but on account of the attention it attracted. An airtel from the Washington Field Office to Hoover on the topic of the 22 April 1967 issue of *The Washington Post and Times Herald* indicated that Clay was due to speak at Howard University.[43] While the Washington Office remarked that Clay would make 'comments regarding Black Power', they emphasised the audience he would be addressing – 'approximately 800 students'. [44] Ali's profile allowed him to inspire demographics that other NOI members could not. The Bureau identified that 'The Champ's main role is to [...] convert them ["Negro youths"] to the Muslim Faith', and by extension to segregationist thought. Furthermore, Ali's utility as a public figure extended beyond American shores, which proved valuable in making friends for the NOI on foreign soil.

During Ali's trip to Ghana, the NOI's news organ reported that 'Africans [...] act as though a dearly beloved friend has returned home, not for a visit'.[45] Given that Ali's patriotism was already in doubt, this would have alarmed Hoover, especially because the FBI had already noted that, before a television audience in 1964, Ali 'called Africa "home"'.[46]

[42] AFBIA 1, 404.

[43] AFBIA 2, 523.

[44] *Ibid.*

[45] Charles P. Howard, 'Africa Opens Arms for Return of Prodigal Son', *Muhammad Speaks*, 19 June 1964, quoted in Gibson, *A History of the Nation of Islam*, 54.

[46] AFBIA 2, 618.

Ali's unique capacity as a NOI member was not limited to publicity. The files demonstrate a concern that Ali assisted the group financially, indicated by the time and energy the Bureau devoted to monitoring Main Bout, Inc. Main Bout was the promotional outfit Ali formed, and which funded the NOI until Ali's 1967 conviction for draft evasion. Hoover issued a memorandum instructing: 'Follow "Main Bout. Inc." and its possible incorporation in New York, and advise Bureau, Chicago, and other interested offices of developments.' [47] Hoover commanded numerous offices to update him on developments, not on account of any suspected unlawful activity, but because 'The NOI will also receive income from receipts of Main Bout'.[48] Agents updated him on every detail, particularly on the finances of Main Bout's 'officers': they reported that the company President, Herbert Muhammad, and Secretary, John Ali, were earning $45,000 and $35,000 per year respectively.[49] Such was the FBI's concern for Ali's economic influence that it recorded an article of 8 February 1967 in the *Chicago Daily News*, which fictitiously detailed that 'CLAY, who fights under the Black Muslim name of MUHAMMAD ALI, is broke', as any reduction in the 'substantial donations made by him to the NOI [might] possibly caus[e] MUHAMMAD to "dump" [redacted passage]'.[50]

The FBI's obsession with Ali far outweighed nearly all other members of the NOI, despite his not even being part of the leadership. As well as Ali's perceived threat as a puppet of the NOI, his prestigious position within boxing had to be

[47] AFBIA 1, 346.
[48] AFBIA 2, 631.
[49] AFBIA 1, 348.
[50] AFBIA 2, 640; AFBIA 1, 430.

considered. The heavyweight champion was 'supposed to stand as a role model for American youth and a symbol of American strength'. [51] However, Ali represented a total subversion of what Hoover deemed to be a great American. A newspaper clipping from the *Chicago Sunday Sun-Times*, entitled 'Cassius Clay', was recorded by the FBI for simply commenting on Ali's forthcoming fight being billed as being for the 'UNDISPUTED world championship'. [52] Given Ali's perceived transgressions, every accolade and belt he accumulated symbolised a black mark against Hoover's America. With such accomplishments, Ali's notability outgrew that of the NOI, underlining that the FBI's investigation was more than just about his membership, but was also to do with Ali the individual.

Eig comments that by 1964 Ali had become 'one of the most famous black men on the planet – possibly *the* most famous'.[53] He was a more visible symbol of the Black Power Movement than the Messenger himself. In the words of Jeremiah Shabazz, 'When Elijah spoke, his words were confined to whatever city he had spoken in. But Ali was a sports hero [...] His voice carried throughout the world.'[54] He featured on talk shows, in the news, 'talk[ing] to people that Elijah Muhammad and Malcolm X never could reach'.[55] The Bureau's Chicago Office directed a letterhead memorandum

[51] Eig, *Ali: A Life*, 216.
[52] Irv Kupcinet, 'Cassius Clay', *Chicago Sunday Sun-Times*, 2 February 1966, in AFBIA 1, 371.
[53] Eig, *Ali: A Life*, 156.
[54] Jeremiah Shabazz as quoted in interview in Thomas Hauser, *Muhammad Ali: His Life and Times* (New York: Simon and Schuster, 1991), 135.
[55] Montville, *Sting Like a Bee*, 69.

to Hoover concerning 'the appearance of CASSIUS CLAY on "Kup's Show" on Channel 7', which indicates its unease over Clay's media appearances.[56] Moreover, the evidence suggests that Ali's star status inadvertently invited an ego-driven investigation from Hoover. Hoover saw Ali as almost 'untouchable', and so may personally have wanted to tarnish his profile as part of a power trip.[57] Despite a lack of hard evidence, Hoover felt it necessary to dedicate resources for thirteen months to investigating alleged match-fixing in Ali's 1965 championship fight with Sonny Liston. Although several FBI officers wrote to Hoover in the following weeks to explain that they 'had heard nothing specific about any "dumping" for this fight', and would close their cases, the Director's office demanded that the investigation continue, providing new reasons that relied solely on idle speculation. [58]

Muhammad Ali defied white expectations of a heavyweight champion. His rebellion stirred confusion, as many wondered, 'Why was he complaining? He was heavyweight champion. This was an exalted position in American culture [...] Why couldn't he be happy? Be normal?'[59] Ali resisted 'normal' standards, which tacitly demanded that an African American feel honoured to have reached the peak of a white-controlled industry. Rather, he sought change for all blacks, responding to the aforementioned questions with, 'I don't have to be what you want me to be.'[60] Through such

---

[56] AFBIA 1, 485.

[57] JPat Brown, 'Even to FBI Director J. Edgar Hoover, Muhammad Ali was "untouchable"', *MuckRock*, 14 December 2017, available at **https://bit.ly/2qjHrok** (accessed 9 December 2017).

[58] AFBIA 2, 709.

[59] Montville, *Sting Like a Bee*, 17.

[60] Robert Lipsyte, 'Clay discusses his future, Liston and Black

declamations, Ali rejected 'the old promise that black people would get a fair chance if they played by the rules'.[61] He tore up the rule-book, showing no respect for the white establishment that Hoover strived to preserve.

Malcolm X, following Ali's win over Liston, told a reporter, 'The power structure had successfully created the image of the American Negro as someone with no confidence, no militancy.'[62] Ali cast aside the role black athletes were meant to play, as nobody could tell him how to speak or act. He stood as a pillar of resistance for African Americans, saying, '"I'm so pretty [...] black is beautiful" before that became fashionable.'[63] Instead of playing up to white officials who historically had run the sport, Ali presented himself as a champion for the oppressed, making the heavyweight championship a vehicle for social mobility. Moreover, by announcing his new business venture, Main Bout, 'Ali was asserting unprecedented autonomy for a black athlete'.[64] It established black independence 'in terms that would have been unimaginable in 1960', a time to which Hoover's mind had possibly not even progressed.[65] The Bureau documented an article written by Olsen that portrayed Ali as racist for saying 'nor are "whiteys" themselves [important to him],

Muslims', *The New York Times*, 27 February 1964, available at **https:// nyti.ms/2rim7WX** (accessed 5 March 2018).

[61] Eig, *Ali: A Life*, 153-4.

[62] *Muhammad Ali: The Whole Story*, directed by Joseph Consentino and Sandra Consentino (1996; Warner Home Video, 2001).

[63] Thomas Hauser, *Thomas Hauser on Boxing: Another Year Inside the Sweet Science* (Fayetteville: University of Arkansas Press, 2014), 151.

[64] Eig, *Ali: A Life*, 207-8.

[65] *Ibid.*, 208.

except insofar as they can further his career'.[66] The agency appeared disturbed by the role reversal Ali manufactured, in which a black athlete was not being manipulated by white businessmen but possibly the reverse.

It also filed a clipping from the *Courier Journal*, dated 30 September 1966, entitled 'Clay's contract will expire one day before bout here'.[67] With no reference to the NOI, it was purely about the termination of Ali's contract with the Louisville Sponsoring Group. It signalled that Ali was breaking from his white promoters, with whom he had signed shortly after (as Cassius Clay) he won the Olympic Games' light heavyweight championship, a moment when to the FBI Ali was America's darling, prior to his challenging of societal structures.[68] The 'degree of racism, or at least paternalism, in the way the Louisville Sponsoring Group treated Ali' brought them closer to the values displayed by the Bureau.[69] Ali's embrace of black economic nationalism likely frightened Hoover: one FBI report detailing a conversation Ali had had concludes with the acknowledgement that 'Negroes could gain recognition in the business world'.[70]

The literature so far produced on the declassified files is not only slim but has presented the FBI's surveillance of Ali largely as a consequence of his membership of the NOI. It was certainly a focal point, with his devotion to Islam ultimately informing Ali's views on race – most notably, his advocacy for

---

[66] Jack Olsen, 'A Case of Conscience', *Sports Illustrated*, 11 April 1966, in AFBIA 1, 419.

[67] Early Ruby, 'Clay's contract will expire one day before bout here', *Courier Journal*, 30 September 1966, in AFBIA 1, 491.

[68] *Ibid.*

[69] Eig, *Ali: A Life*, 199.

[70] AFBIA 2, 638.

black separation and self-defence – but these became more significant in generating FBI concern. The agents' allusion to such views and the Honourable Elijah's book, *Message to the Blackman*, supports Jeffreys-Jones's thesis that race underpinned the Bureau's COINTELPRO activities. However, while the Bureau originally claimed that 'Clay is a member of the Nation of Islam [redacted passage] but he is not the subject of an active investigation' the FBI in fact recorded Ali's movements and activities obsessively, more than those of nearly any other NOI member.[71] One reason is that Ali was able to aid the group financially and help its membership grow. Moreover, he occupied the position of heavyweight champion, which, unlike any other in sports in the period, transcended merely local or national audiences and had global recognition. In one article that the FBI recorded, Olsen wrote, 'Europeans may never have heard of America's Koufax, and North Americans may know little about Brazil's Pele [...] but who doesn't know who the heavyweight champion is?'[72] He subverted contemporary expectations of this paramount role by not playing the obedient 'negro' and not abiding by the rules implicitly set out by the white institution.

[71] AFBIA 1, 412.
[72] Olsen, 'A Case of Conscience', in AFBIA 1, 425.

Chapter 3

'I don't have no personal quarrel with those Viet Congs': Ali's draft refusal and the anti-war movement

Muhammad Ali's non-conforming views on race and religion aroused concern both within and outside of the Bureau. However, it was his decision to refuse his draft induction that represented the ultimate insult to much white American sentiment. A chronological examination of the files highlights an escalation of surveillance in accordance with Ali's mounting draft resistance.

When Ali first emerged into celebrity, David Remnick reasons that he conformed to the 'Good Negro' stereotype, leaving no doubt about his patriotic values as he confirmed, 'the U.S.A is still the best country in the world'.[1] Moreover, when America joined the war in 1965, Ali was 'happy to avoid talking about the army or Vietnam at all'.[2] However, his passivity declined and the FBI reciprocated with heightened surveillance, viewing Ali's defiance as a slight against American standards and a threat to American interests.

Ali's NOI-involvement was even more problematic with regard to the draft than it was concerning religion and racial politics. As the Vietnam War escalated, Ali's affiliation stoked fears that he might evade the draft, as 'In the past, officials and members of the NOI, including MUHAMMAD, have refused to register'.[3] The NOI had a history of draft refusals: the Messenger himself 'had served four years in prison during

[1] Cassius Clay quoted in David Remnick, *King of the World: Muhammad Ali and the Rise of the American Hero* (New York: Picador, 1999), 104.

[2] Hauser, *Muhammad Ali*, 142-3.

[3] AFBIA 1, 495.

World War II for refusing to fight'.[4] These anxieties were also responsible for the meticulous watch over Ali's position in the NOI. The SAC, Louisville, cautioned Hoover that Ali had 'been claiming to be a minister in the NOI in order to avoid military service'.[5] Moreover, the Bureau chronicled an article which appeared in the 23 August 1966 issue of the *Louisville Times*, which speculated that Ali's attorney would file with the draft board 'a petition for reopening the entire case and reclassifying CLAY as a minister'.[6] The FBI's emphasis on Ali's draft suggests that it was less about gaining information about the NOI and their use of Ali, than Ali's potential use of the NOI to avoid enlistment. Following Ali's 27 February 1964 announcement of his NOI membership, his failed pre-induction mental exam a month later received far greater attention. It led many to presume that he had 'taken a dive on the test to avoid service'.[7] A *New York Times* article published within a week of Ali's test underlines the incredulity felt by many Americans that a man so articulate failed an examination in which a score of only 30 out of 100 was required to pass.[8] Moreover, it spotlights the basic questions posed: 'A man works from 6 in the morning to 3 in the afternoon with 1 hour for lunch. How many hours did he work? a) 7 b) 8...'.[9]

Two years after Ali had failed the Armed Forces qualifying

[4] Eig, *Ali: A Life*, 214.

[5] AFBIA 2, 533.

[6] *Ibid.*, 627.

[7] Eig, *Ali: A Life*, 162.

[8] Jack Raymond, 'Cassius Clay Rejected by Army', *The New York Times*, 21 March 1964, available at **https://nyti.ms/2HYzuTr** (accessed 16 March 2018).

[9] *Ibid.*

test, the Vietnam War had escalated and so his situation bore greater significance. From 1964 to 1965, the number of American soldiers dying yearly in Vietnam increased more than nine-fold, from around 200 to 1,900.[10] In 1966, the death toll tripled to more than 6,000 and 'generals at the Pentagon now wanted more than 400,000 troops for the war effort'.[11] In response, the FBI recorded coverage pertaining to Ali's draft status. For instance, agents in Chicago forwarded 'Kup's Column' from an edition of the *Chicago Sun-Times* in January 1966, which reported that the U.S. government was 'considering a re-evaluation of the draft status of CASSIUS CLAY'.[12] Hoover was appalled by Ali's 1-Y draftee status and when, in early 1966, the armed forces lowered its standards to permit soldiers above the fifteenth percentile, and Ali was again classified as 1-A, the FBI's eagerness to inform Hoover was reflected by a teletype of 23 February 1966, headed 'URGENT', notifying that Ali 'HAS BEEN DRAFTED'.[13] The aim of its surveillance transformed correspondingly, its attention now being tuned to any indication that Ali would resist. The agency noted Ali's remarks at a NOI convention in late February 1966 as being 'against the nation's military endeavours in Vietnam', emphasising the apprehension that Ali might refuse the draft.[14]

On 28 February 1966, eleven days after being notified of his new draft status, Ali took his opposition to the war into the public sphere by submitting paperwork claiming to be a

[10] Eig, *Ali: A Life*, 211.

[11] Montville, *Sting Like a Bee*, 11.

[12] AFBIA 1, 382.

[13] *Ibid.*, 370.

[14] Edmund J. Rooney, 'FBI Watches Black Muslim, Cassius Clay', *Louisville Times*, 28 February 1966, in AFBIA 1, 354.

conscientious objector. The FBI monitored his religious objections as Ali questioned, 'why should he, as a Muslim, be forced into the Army'.[15] Ali outlined his racial opposition too, demanding to know why he should represent the U.S. abroad 'while so-called Negro people in Louisville are treated like dogs and denied simple human rights?'[16]

However, the Bureau did not seem to care about Ali's motivation as much as the consequence of his un-American actions. As such, Hoover kept a close eye on Ali's various fights in this period. In the prelude to Ali's bout with Ernie Terrell in Chicago on 29 March 1966, the boxer indicated to the press that he would refuse to serve. The Miami SAC alerted Hoover that it was while 'training for his scheduled fight with ERNIE TERRELL [... that] he made his comment about service', and so the fight temporarily became the hub of their investigation.[17] The FBI was against the bout taking place, and noted favourably a newspaper report which claimed that Illinois Governor Otto Kerner had 'wrapped himself in the American flag [...] branding Cassius Clay unpatriotic and ordering the bout banished from the unblemished state'.[18] The evocative 'banished' likens Ali to a traitor, while 'unblemished' lends a sense of purity that is at odds with Ali's 'treason'. The Bureau was pleased that the Illinois State Athletic Commission acquiesced and cancelled the match, but with the possibility that Ali might fight elsewhere, they recorded an article in the *Louisville Courier Journal* 'showing the various US locations that wanted no

[15] AFBIA 2, 525.
[16] Mike Marqusee, *Redemption Song: Muhammad Ali and the Spirit of the Sixties* (London: Verso, 2000), 213-15.
[17] AFBIA 1, 414.
[18] *Ibid.*, 385.

part of the title bout between Muhammad Ali and Terrell'.[19] Ali eventually fought in Canada, his travel there permitted by the Louisville Draft Board on account of its proximity to the United States. However, while the FBI filed an article that uttered 'good riddance' to Ali, Hoover was clearly concerned that Ali might desert.[20] For the fight with Henry Cooper in London, he tracked Ali's travel arrangements in the city on 3 May 1966. Robert Lipsyte asserts that Hoover 'didn't want to risk his staying in Europe to avoid the draft'.[21] An airtel to Hoover confirms the assumption, as it is especially attentive to details on Ali's 'return flight' on their '14-day excursion'.[22]

Crucially, the majority of Americans in 1966 still supported the effort to fight communism in southeast Asia, and as the death count in Vietnam rose, many felt that 'if South Vietnam fell to a communist power, the rest of southeast Asia would follow'. [23] Hoover was receptive to public opinion and, while never explicitly labelling Ali a communist, the files intimate that they saw him as complicit in its spread. Following the Ali-Terrell fight's migration from the U.S.A. to Canada, General Lewis B. Hershey, who headed the Selective Service System, said, 'I hope that Carl Braden of Communist fame can accompany the Muhammud [sic] Ali to Montreal as his protector.'[24] While not saying that Ali was a

[19] *Ibid.*

[20] *Ibid.*

[21] R. Lipsyte, *Free to Be Muhammad Ali* (New York: Bantam Books, 1979), 85.

[22] AFBIA 1, 440.

[23] Eig, *Ali: A Life*, 211.

[24] AFBIA 1, 385. Carl Braden was a white Louisville journalist and civil rights activist who had twice been imprisoned for his activism in support of black equality. He had refused to cooperate with the

communist, Hershey and the FBI wilfully associated him with a suspected communist. Moreover, the Bureau was suspicious of the NOI giving financial support to Kwame Nkrumah of Ghana, whose relationship with the communist world was well known.[25] Given Hoover's 'paranoid style', the information that Nkrumah had 'received CASSIUS CLAY and HERBERT MUHAMMAD at the official Ghanese residence warmly', would have reinforced connections between Ali and communism. [26] Lastly, the FBI made note of a letter, personally addressed to Hoover from an ex-serviceman, in which he complained about Ali being allowed to urge different groups 'to disregard their call for service'. Most pertinently, he called for Hoover to 'put Clay and Carmichael on a one-way ticket to Russia', insinuating that Ali was acting like a communist. [27] Montville comments that World War II veterans were not a forgiving group.[28]

Ali himself even said, 'They say we're Communists. That is not true', indicating the ideological suspicions aroused by NOI draft refusals. [29] However, the FBI files were more focused upon Ali's alleged lack of patriotism, a core value upheld by the Bureau. According to an airgram from Egypt, on 9 July 1964, Ali was shown a film on his visit there which depicted the 1956 attack on Port Said. It was deemed to be of interest because Ali was quoted as saying that 'the U. S. press

House Un-American Activities Committee in 1961.

[25] AFBIA 3, 508.

[26] Timothy Melley, *Empire of Conspiracy: The Culture of Paranoia in Postwar America* (Ithaca, NY: Cornell University Press, 2000), 2; *Ibid.*

[27] AFBIA 2, 539.

[28] Montville, *Sting Like a Bee*, 19.

[29] Eig, *Ali: A Life*, 155.

tried to make it appear as an Arab aggression against Israel' and that if such aggression took place now, Ali 'should have been pleased to fight on your side and under your flag'.[30] Ali not only scorned the American press, but seemingly demonstrated a willingness to take up arms for a foreign country while not defending his own.

Hoover saw the boxer as the antagonist to the American civil religion, which demanded that its citizens help defend it against its enemies. His own nationalism was expounded in a letter from an unnamed correspondent, pressing Hoover to 'strip Clay of all his wealth and let people see what it means to defy one's country', and lauding Hoover's values: 'Unamerican? Not on your beloved head...'.[31] Hoover not only deemed the letter to be worthy of filing, but felt sufficient sympathy to issue a reply expressing gratitude and apology. His tone was remorseful, saying that he 'want[s] to assure you that we in the FBI are well aware of our responsibilities', and that he was dismayed that the FBI 'does not determine if prosecution will be instituted in any situation', having to refer its investigations to the U.S. Department of Justice.[32]

Nonetheless, any opportunity that did arise for the incarceration of the draft-dodging Ali, the agency wilfully took, such as the 'smuggling violation' in which Ali had allegedly failed to declare upon his return to the U.S. jewellery he had purchased in Germany.[33] In February 1967, close to the climax of Ali's draft case, the prospect of actually arresting him for something that was illegal would probably have felt like a major payoff. The FBI unsparingly obliged in helping

[30] AFBIA 3, 257.
[31] AFBIA 2, 536.
[32] *Ibid.*, 535.
[33] *Ibid.*, 517.

the Bureau of Customs determine the location of Ali: with their 'top echelon informant coverage of the NOI, we are attempting to locate him'.[34]

Ali's position within boxing, as was true of his views on religion and race, intensified the FBI's reaction to his draft refusal. In seeming puzzlement, Ali declared that he could not understand 'why out of all the baseball players, all of the football players, all of the basketball players – they seek out me, who's the world's only heavyweight champion?' [35] However, he had inadvertently answered his own question: he was world champion and was expected to set an example, in this case a pro-Vietnam War example. During the Second World War, Joe Louis had volunteered for U.S. army service and 'his willingness to serve and his patriotism reassured whites about the loyalty of black Americans'. [36] It was anticipated that someone in Ali's position would act similarly, and could have served in a ceremonial capacity, as Louis had, visiting and entertaining troops. Benjamin T. Harrison points out that Ali, as an international celebrity, would have been expected to follow in the footsteps of previous champions like Louis and Sugar Ray Robinson, who had both served in the U.S. Army.[37]

Paul Beston's revisionist history, seemingly reflecting

[34] *Ibid.*, 518.

[35] 'Clay Sees Self as Boon to U.S. in Civilian Dress', *Chicago Tribune*, 21 February 1966, quoted in Michael Ezra, 'Main Bout, Inc., Black Economic Power, and Professional Boxing: The Cancelled Muhammad Ali/Ernie Terrell Fight', *Journal of Sport History* 29, 3 (2002), 418.

[36] Timothy L. Reed, 'Peace profile: Muhammad Ali', *Peace Review* 16, 1 (2004), 108.

[37] Harrison, 'The Muhammad Ali Draft Case', 70.

critical contemporary opinions, asserts that 'Had Ali chosen more wisely, he might have become a unifier, like Louis.'[38] This argument has limited validity in that, while Louis may have helped break down some inherent biases in the soldiers he entertained, he did little to resolve prejudice in America more broadly. Moreover, Louis was acting in a very different America, during the 1940s, compared to that of 1967. While Beston's critique may be a 'feeble attempt to re-write history', it is reflective of white American opinion contemporaneous with Ali's draft refusal.[39] Rather than fulfil this supposed role of 'unifier', Ali acted conversely, becoming a symbol of and rallying point for opposition to the draft and the Vietnam War.

Ali stated, 'I don't have no personal quarrel with those Viet Congs', building upon his insistence that his enemy was not in southeast Asia, but was American racism. [40] Later, a variation on these words would be widely attributed to him: 'I ain't got no quarrel with the Viet Cong', which became the defining slogan of Ali's anti-war stance. While to some it smacked of treason and dissent, to others it had a ring of common sense. Ali's draft refusal consequently promoted public debate on the Vietnam War during a time when 'the government was desperately trying to prevent that dis-

[38] Paul Beston, 'The Truth About Muhammad Ali and the Draft', *Wall Street Journal*, 28 April 2017, available at **https://bit.ly/2HOKoMo** (accessed 5 March 2018).

[39] Anonymous, '"The Truth about Muhammad Ali and the Draft" – Wall Street Journal Op-ed Shamelessly Smears an Icon', 29 April 2017, available at **https://bit.ly/2Kxdhww** (accessed 23 March 2018).

[40] Montville, *Sting Like a Bee*, 23.

course'.[41] The picture that Lyndon Johnson's government portrayed was that of innocent South Vietnamese democrats being unjustly attacked, while 'the United States acted as the sheriff's posse riding to the rescue'.[42] Ali undermined this foreign policy narrative and 'became a symbol of the belief that, unless there's a very good reason for killing people, war is wrong'.[43] He challenged the violence that American nationalist sentiment was demanding, urging pacifism instead.

Hoover, alarmed by Ali's public stand, had informants at meetings in 1968 where Ali 'talked at length on the war in Vietnam'.[44] Through such meetings, Ali was able to 'educate Americans on the war, and the opposition to the war increased'.[45] He drew the country's attention to the fact that black men were dying at a starkly disproportionate rate, accounting for twenty-two per cent of all battlefield deaths when the black population in America was only ten per cent.[46] While the black press initially castigated Ali, expressing their 'regret that Clay has chosen not to bear arms for his country', the racial injustice he brought into public consciousness gradually reversed opinions.[47] The Bureau exhibited their

[41] Harrison, 'The Muhammad Ali Draft Case', 69.

[42] R. M. Fisher, *Rhetoric and American Democracy: Black Protest Through Vietnam Dissent* (Lanham, MD: University Press of America, 1985), 220.

[43] Hauser, *Thomas Hauser on Boxing*, 151.

[44] AFBIA 3, 1061.

[45] Harrison, 'The Muhammad Ali Draft Case', 72-3.

[46] Eig, *Ali: A Life*, 228.

[47] Frank L. Stanley, 'Is Religion a Last Resort?', *Louisville Defender*, 24 February 1966, quoted in Townsend, 'Shifting Perceptions of Muhammad Ali', 632.

concern, monitoring Ali's emotive racial rhetoric: 'Hold it, stupid! We don't lynch niggers like that nowadays – we can draft them and get the same results.'[48] With such statements, Ali severely dented Hoover's crusade against communism by drawing attention to the unequal distribution of draftees.

When Ali first condemned the war, sentiment against him had steadily risen. However, it has been argued that by 1967 white people saw Ali as the underdog who had been 'fighting alone against an unjust system, and thereby turned public opinion in his favour'. [49] The growth of the anti-war movement was mirrored by increased FBI surveillance of Ali, as prominent civil rights leaders joined his cause. According to a memorandum marked 'secret', Ali and Martin Luther King, Jr. met privately for approximately thirty minutes, and their talk 'mainly consisted of joking and "horse play"'.[50] The Bureau bugged the meeting, and felt the need to transcribe the conversation, especially as King had been rigid in his refusal to adopt Ali's stand until this point. Eig comments that this meeting 'reflected the manner in which the civil rights movement and the anti-war movement were colliding'.[51]

Civil rights leaders were frequent targets of COINTELPRO, and for Ali to unite with them within an even more problematic movement may have been Hoover's greatest fear. Indeed, just days after their meeting, King called the U.S. 'the greatest purveyor of violence in the world

[48] Jack Olsen, 'A Case of Conscience', *Sports Illustrated*, 11 April 1966, in AFBIA 1, 420.

[49] Gardell, *In the Name of Elijah Muhammad*, 68.

[50] Report, 6 February 1968, Herbert Muhammad FBI File, Malcolm X Manning Marable Collection, quoted in Eig, *Ali: A Life*, 195.

[51] Eig, *Ali: A Life*, 238.

today', expressing the compulsion he felt to condemn the war. [52] The ever-growing number of anti-war protests Ali inspired infuriated Hoover and, as a direct consequence, the FBI watched Ali's house in Chicago, according to Ali's cousin, Charlotte Waddell. She claimed that FBI agents approached her and pleaded for her help in gathering information. [53]

With regard to most of its files, the FBI claimed to be monitoring Ali solely for information on the 'subversive' NOI. However, it was ultimately his draft refusal that altered its official stand, and Ali became 'the current subject of a Bureau investigation under Selective Service Act, 1948', which centred around increasing the strength of the United States' armed forces. [54] Moreover, a report by the agency was part of the required legal process when someone asked to be classified as a conscientious objector, as Ali did in 1966. The FBI compiled a thirty-one-page report, which was submitted to Local Draft Board No. 47 on 9 July 1966. Thirty-five interviews were conducted with both named and unnamed sources. To qualify as a conscientious objector, the draft registrant had to prove that his objection was based on an unwavering sincerity in his religious beliefs. However, the report on Ali 'was more extensive than anything most of the 170,000 applicants for conscientious objector status between 1965 and 1970 would ever receive', reinforcing the impression of Ali's importance as heavyweight champion and a public symbol. [55] The Bureau produced a singular, flat narrative, largely stripped of nuance. The term 'brainwashed' was regularly employed, and the FBI interviewed family members

[52] *Ibid.*, 239.
[53] *Ibid.*, 249.
[54] AFBIA 2, 518.
[55] Montville, *Sting Like a Bee*, 62.

who undermined the sincerity of his religious convictions. For instance, Ali's mother, Odessa O'Grady Clay, insisted that she 'raised CASSIUS as a member of the Baptist faith'.[56] The FBI also sought evidence to suggest that Ali was a violent individual outside of boxing, despite his insistence that he was a pacifist. It asked an unnamed associate about an article which appeared in a local Miami newspaper 'which reported CLAY had purchased a .22 caliber Derringer gun'. However, he assured them that 'this was the only gun or weapon' Ali had ever owned.[57]

Hoover often resorted to 'unsavoury practices [aimed at] discomforting and persecuting some of those regarded by him as enemies of American society', and nothing sculpted Ali into a greater opponent than his draft refusal.[58] Hoover's boys devoted more attention to Ali's draft than to any other matter within these files. Moreover, a chronological trend can definitely be observed: the Bureau extended its surveillance of Ali the more his anti-war stance became explicit. It began with his failed mental exam, and was followed by the Bureau's suspicions about Ali acting as a minister in preparation for seeking conscientious objector status, all the while being fuelled by the escalation of the war. His tempering of black martial pride through reference to the racial inequity of enlistment, and finally his becoming a symbol of the anti-war movement as the cruelty of the war began to touch the conscience of black and white Americans alike, was what turned Ali into a prime focus of FBI surveillance.

[56] AFBIA 2, 597.
[57] *Ibid.*, 600.
[58] Karg, 'Review Article: *The Bureau*', 72.

Conclusion

In a country that had begun to 'push and pull itself apart with the assassination of John F. Kennedy on November 22, 1963, with all different voices and sects arguing for different futures' for America, Ali stood at one extreme, as a figure of controversy.[1] During the years that followed, the FBI placed the boxer under surveillance, which it claimed was owing to his relationship with the Nation of Islam. However, I have argued that the Bureau's motivation for monitoring Ali was actually multi-faceted. Hoover's personal anxiety over Ali's religious and racial attitudes was also intensified by his activity outside of the NOI, which contradicted Hoover's notion of how a respectable heavyweight champion should conduct himself. The chief cause, however, was Ali's draft refusal, his most explicit challenge to mainstream expectations. Ali represented 'a multiple signifier of opposition' to Hoover's socio-political vision.[2]

This multi-causal explanation for FBI surveillance posits Ali's notoriety as an undercurrent. The Bureau identified that Ali's chief value to the NOI was 'the publicity he brings this organisation and the funds he contributed to it'.[3] The release of the FBI papers shows that Hoover demonstrated little discrimination over intelligence sources, demanding every detail be documented, even if it were wildly speculative. It is therefore simplistic to imagine that Ali would have been monitored so obsessively without the fame that his accomplishments inside the ring delivered. The NOI 'hardly

[1] Montville, *Sting Like a Bee*, 16.

[2] Robin D. G. Kelley, 'The Riddle of the Zoot: Malcolm Little and Black Cultural Politics during WWII', quoted in Gorn (ed.), *Muhammad Ali*, 42.

[3] AFBIA 1, 477.

represented a communist threat. The FOI soldiers couldn't be seriously judged as capable of overthrowing the contemporary power structure in the United States.'[4] Therefore the threat that Ali represented must be understood at another level. As I have stressed, Ali's actions must be seen in the context of the ideology of 'Americanity' or the 'American civil religion'.[5] Instead of embracing the U.S.A. as the greatest country, and Americans as the 'chosen people', Ali challenged the status quo by fundamentally criticising the morality of the Vietnam war and, in so doing, called into question his own allegiance to 'the flag'.

At just twenty-four years of age, Ali was 'the most widely recognised athlete on earth, the most prominent Muslim in America, and the most visible opponent of the war in Vietnam'.[6] Eig's tricolon is mimetic of Ali's mounting challenge to America, as Hoover saw it, building towards his draft case. Consequently, the release of the FBI files on Ali represents a major contribution to the existing primary source material available on the Bureau. While 'No civilian government agency in the United States has received as much attention from authors', scholars have yet to explore adequately its relationship with certain individuals, as many files still remained classified.[7] However, although the files on Ali are incomplete, in that they incorporate deletions which protect confidential sources and have many pages missing, it is still possible to produce a telling and nuanced explanation of why federal agents surveilled and recorded the boxer's life, and how this reflects on the FBI.

[4] Gardell, *In the Name of Elijah Muhammad*, 93.

[5] Gardell, *In the Name of Elijah Muhammad*, 93.

[6] Eig, *Ali: A Life*, 228

[7] Vizzard, 'The FBI', 1079.